DEATH AND THE LIFE TO COME

GW00690058

THE FOUNDATIONS SERIES

The Foundations series, published in association with the Evangelical Alliance, covers aspects of everyday life and faith crucial to today's Christian. Each book addresses a different theme and defines what evangelical Christians believe, and why. Topics include the Bible, evangelism, prayer, guidance, evangelicalism and miracles.

'Thought-provoking and faith-building, this series of Christian basics should be read widely.' *Clive Calver*

Other titles in the Foundations series

DEATH AND THE LIFE TO COME

Ian Barclay

HODDER AND STOUGHTON
LONDON SYDNEY AUCKLAND TORONTO

British Library Cataloguing in Publication Data

Barclay, Ian
   Death and the life to come.
   1. Death – Christian viewpoints
   I. Title   II. Series
   248.4

ISBN 0 340 42633 0

Hodder & Stoughton Editorial Office: 47 Bedford Square, London WC1B 3DP.

CONTENTS

Introduction

THE WAY OUT

In the film *Chariots of Fire* Eric Liddell is the central figure, but the story also touches on the life of Harold Abrahams, a Cambridge athletics blue and Olympic gold medallist. While Eric Liddell became a missionary in the Far East, Harold Abrahams joined the BBC.

The trouble Harold Abrahams took in preparing for a broadcast became legendary. Brian Johnston once illustrated Abrahams' meticulous attention to detail by referring to a little booklet he had produced. Johnston writes, 'It was typical of his love of detail and must have involved much journeying to and fro on the Underground. The booklet showed where all the "Way Out" signs were situated on every London tube station, and the number of the carriage which always stopped exactly opposite the exit.'

One word the Bible uses for death is

exodus, which means 'the way out'. In this book in the Foundations Series, I want to look at the emotional, biblical, physical and Christian experience of death, so that when a member of our family or a friend dies, we will know what is happening to them and to us. I also hope it will be used to give away to friends and neighbours when they ask about 'death and the life to come'.

It would be hard to attempt to write a book like this without some experience of the matter. My first wife died seven years ago after battling with cancer for nine years. As an Anglican clergyman, I had often tried to help other people in their loss and had taken hundreds of funeral services, but it wasn't until Sheila's death that I understood something of the trauma involved. Those who suffer this way are called 'bereaved', coming from the word 'reave' meaning 'to ravage, rob and leave desolate'. It is out of this experience that I write. I want to try and make bereavement understandable and bearable for those who go through it, as well as providing a helpful summary of the basic Christian teaching on death and the life to come.

Hove 1988   Ian Barclay

1

SORROW COMES TO EVERYBODY

The Emotional Experience of Death

Grief and *sorrow* are nearly always the first aspects of death to touch us. Although it is possible to live through to middle age without having to face death in our family or circle of friends, eventually it will happen and we will be confronted with the perplexing experience of bereavement. In the British Isles 800,000 people die every year. One day inevitably we will be part of those figures, and before that time they must include members of our family and some of our close friends.

We need to prepare ourselves by trying to understand the subject as fully as possible, always allowing the final limitation that complete knowledge can't be ours until we experience the event.

What is grief?

Grief is an emotional wound with several recognisable symptoms. Colin Parkes describes it thus: 'When a love-tie is severed, an emotional and behavioural reaction is set in train which we call grief.' He goes on to say, 'Newly bereaved people are often surprised and frightened by the sheer intensity of their sorrows.'

A grief observed

Every experience of grief is deeply personal and highly individual. It would be impossible to list the symptoms we will feel or to place them in the order in which they will come. No two experiences of grief are the same, because the people and circumstances involved are always different. However, if you stop to map out a time of grief after it has happened, there are patterns of behaviour and emotions that are similar.

Tears Crying is a mechanism which the body uses to release tension. If we are a typical English male we may have tried to suppress tears with a stiff upper lip. In the ordinary events of life, tears can also be suppressed by deliberately choosing laughter to ease tension. In everyday experiences the emotional adjustments are small, but in bereavement they can be of mountainous proportions. At such times the body will often choose tears as an emergency safety valve. During these times crying can be as uncontrollable as it is unwanted.

Jim Graham, the pastor of Goldhill Baptist Church, tells of how he received news in Singapore of his father's death, a death which, because of recent ill health, was not entirely unexpected. The Grahams were leaving for the Philippines the next morning and so decided to go out for a meal with friends as planned. Jim Graham continues, 'I had just closed the door behind us as we made our way to the restaurant for our meal, when I was suddenly, unexpectedly and publicly overwhelmed with tears. They shook me quite uncontrollably – and I felt so foolish and terribly embarrassed and exposed.' That is typical of what can happen at a time of bereavement.

Anger Elizabeth Heike, a committed Christian, tells of how, after the death of a friend who had had a terminal illness, she was angry with God. 'It had taken me all my time to face the fact that I was angry at all, but to be angry with Him who had shown me so much· of His love during Madelien's illness and after her death seemed ungrateful and a denial of the reality of that experience.'

Jesus was also angry about death. At the grave of Lazarus we are told He was 'deeply moved in his spirit and troubled'. Another version says 'He gave way to such distress of spirit as made his body tremble'. The words imply not only that he experienced grief, but also intense anger at the unnaturalness of death. Death wasn't part of God's original plan: it came as a direct result of man's sin. Jesus seems repelled at the whole idea of the death of a very dear friend.

We mustn't be surprised if someone, in the confusion of grief, says, 'Why has God allowed this to happen to me?' The Bible is clear in its answer. It is the sinfulness of man which has brought death into the world. It can only be confused thinking to lay the responsibility for it at God's door, because He offers eternal life through His Son. Yet anger remains part of grief and it can be vented on God, the minister, the family or a friend, and we must be understanding when we see it.

Shock and numbness When told that her husband had been killed in an accident at work one woman fainted. When she came round she wanted to know what had happened, and when told she fainted again. In all she fainted five times before she could receive the information without reacting violently. Some people can be literally struck dumb with grief, while others are just numb, unable to take in what has happened. Until they do, they live in a dazed and dream-like state, quite unable to think clearly.

Fantasy This happens at two quite different levels. For some days and even weeks after bereavement a few people 'see' their lost loved one in a crowd. It is almost as though the brain is scanning for a familiar image but once the crowd comes into sharp focus the fantasy image disappears.

At another level the fantasy becomes a rejection of reality. Here, there is the irrational belief that the death hasn't happened. A place will be set at the dining-room table, and a room will constantly be prepared for the loved one's return. In all experiences of grief, gentle and comforting counsel is essential. Where there is a loss of reality, professional help must be sought.

Guilt As an Anglican minister I can't remember counselling anyone going through grief without finding that guilt was also involved. I've often heard a husband or a wife say 'If only we had taken that last holiday together', or a grown man say 'If only I had been a more considerate son'. Guilt is the most natural reaction when we lose someone we love, and we must expect it and recognise it when it comes. The human condition and the failure that it brings mean that we can never be the people that we would like to be. When someone is alive, we can pretend that we are better than we are. In a very stark way death can obliterate the memory of the joys we may have given in a relationship, and we remember only the failures and shortcomings. If, after reflection, we are still aware of failure, then we must confess it and roll our burden, as Peter suggests, on to the shoulders of our God who is able to bear it in a way that our human frame can't (1 Peter 5:7).

Exhaustion There will be tiredness. A bereaved person referring to the 'feeling of being utterly drained and exhausted' went on to say, 'This is hardly surprising, for grief is a work and most of our energy will be required to do it. Deep in our minds and spirits, emotions and thoughts must be encountered, experienced and worked through.' Someone else said that the sheer tiredness of grief didn't begin to lift until there had been over a year of relaxed, normal sleep.

How long will grief last?

The important thing is not to anticipate the length of time, but to recognise that we must deal with grief at our own pace. It can't be run against someone else's timetable. There will be tides that ebb and flow, but we are probably talking of about a year for the first step on the road to recovery. Some people find anniversaries extremely difficult to cope with, and they can be traumatic times for many years.

The need to talk

'Give sorrow words' is an important piece of advice. In *The Lament*, Anton Chekhov tells the story of Iona Potapov whose son had died. No one seemed willing to listen to him, and, finally, to find relief he poured out the whole sad story to his horse. The story is powerful because it is so real. Part of the healing process of grief is being able to talk, and not to do so can mean that the healing process can't even begin.

There are those exceptional cases where people just need someone to sit with them. Beethoven wasn't a man known for his social graces. His deafness meant that conversation was often difficult. When he heard of the death of a friend's son, he hurried over to the house to give comfort. Finding a piano in the room, he sat down and played for half an hour, pouring out his love and concern through the music. When he had finished he left without saying a word. Later the friend said that no other visit had been so beneficial.

Whether the reaction is crying, the need to talk, anger or fear, it must come out and be dealt with in a natural way. Any suppressed or repressed feeling will ultimately cause problems until it is dealt with.

What else can I do?

There are practical things that can be done. Hobbies and creative interests are right for some, while others find it a help to do ordinary everyday things, such as a piece of home-decorating, pottering in the garden or cleaning the car.

The Scriptures saved my life

Oliver Cromwell was plunged into utter despair and misery when his son Robert died at the early age of seventeen. Twenty years later he said that Philippians 4:13 ('I can do everything through Him who gives me strength') 'once saved me when my eldest son died, which went as a dagger to my heart.' Bereavement strikes like a dagger and many have found comfort in the Bible. There is one relationship that transcends death and that is the one that we can have with God, which is fed and strengthened by the Bible. The calming words of the Psalms or the words of Jesus to His disciples nourish the soul, and bereavement is a time when the soul can feel particularly dry. There are a number of good aids to understanding the Bible, such as *Every Day With Jesus* or the notes produced by the Scripture Union. Your local Christian bookshop will help.

Learning to live again

As with all wounds, grief eventually heals. For some the process takes longer, but for all of us time is a good medicine and normal life will eventually return. Like most wounds there will be a scar which will never disappear. It wouldn't be right if loved ones were completely forgotten. How could they be?

Gradually, when the trauma has passed and the threads of life are taken up again, the wonderful creativity of our God is such that He can bring a new wholeness into our lives, even new relationships. That is my own experience.

When Sheila died, I suppose, like any man in his late forties, I felt that I would have to settle down to life alone. In a very short time I met Hazel. At first I was frightened of being disloyal to my previous marriage by appearing to believe that someone could easily take Sheila's place. Then I realised that could never happen, but what I was being offered was a completely new relationship, and in no way to be compared with the first. I will never forget Sheila, but I now wonder at the creativity of God, who can restore life by giving someone new to love, which after all is a very basic human need.

2

DEATH IS A THOROUGHFARE

*The Words Used in the
Bible to Describe Death*

It may sound rather depressing to open a Bible and trace the meaning of words such as 'death' and 'dying', but the reverse is true. Not only is it revealing, but it is also quite fascinating to see the writers struggling within the limitations of human language to describe something that will take them and us beyond the grave.

Death is a thoroughfare

There are one or two words in the New Testament that have a twentieth-century ring about them and suggest that man's life can come to an abrupt end. But these are very rare. The most frequently used words speak of the physical, material part of man, that is his body, being separated from the spiritual part, that is his soul. The thrust of the New Testament is that 'Death is a thoroughfare, not a blind alley,' as Victor Hugo put it.

It isn't that some people go down the road of death and emerge in heaven while others get no further than the grave. Death is a thoroughfare down which all men and women make their way. Some will do it unwillingly, but the same life-force that brought us into this world will propel us into the next. This must be the thought in the apostle Peter's mind when he speaks about his 'departure' (2 Peter 1:15). The Greek word is *exodus*, which as well as being the title for the second book of the Bible, is also a description of its contents, namely the exit or exodus of the Hebrew people from the land of Egypt. In the most basic terms the story of the exodus is the history of people moving from one place to another.

Eternity in the minds of men

Most civilisations and cultures have a strong belief in life after death. The Bible teaches us to expect this: Solomon says that God 'has also set eternity in the hearts of men' (Ecclesiastes 3:11). In the creation story we are told that 'God breathed *lives* into man' (a literal translation of Genesis 2:7), the word for 'life' in the original is in the plural. Eternity is not only put within man's intellectual grasp, but he also has an in-built mechanism preparing him for the experience.

Once we look back into history we find that ancient man was certainly aware of eternity. One of the earliest books available is called *The Book of the Dead,* a collection of prayers and formulae whereby the dead might communicate and find their way about. It is interesting that the oldest known name for a coffin, again coming from ancient Egypt, is 'a chest of the living'.

Beyond the exit

Although it cannot be taken as an exact parallel, the book of Exodus can be used as a picture of all that happens to us when we leave this world. The people of Israel, having made their exodus from Egypt, found two further areas before them, the wilderness and the promised land. For them, these two experiences were consecutive. They had to pass through one to enjoy the other. For every person who leaves this world there are two similar areas before them but they are not experienced consecutively. As we go down the thoroughfare called death, we will see either the scenery of the wilderness or the promised land. It will be one or the other, but not both.

The wilderness

The Bible uses two main words to describe the experience we summarise in English as 'hell'. Both have the idea of a wilderness. The first, found in the Old Testament, is the Hebrew word *'Sheol'*: simply the place of the departed. *Sheol* is a grey pit, a shadowy place, where men move about in ghostly form in an environment entirely devoid of colour and joy. The main New Testament word is *'Gehenna'* which paints the frightening picture of Ge Hinnom, Jerusalem's large rubbish dump and public incinerator tucked away from sight in the Valley of Hinnom. Ge Hinnom was a desolate place that perpetually smouldered, where the rubbish and the heat caused a particularly unpleasant species of worm to live and breed rapidly.

Both the pit of Sheol and the Valley of Hinnom suggest places that are hidden away, silent and colourless in the depths of the earth and from which there is no escape. This would seem to be confirmed by our Anglo-Saxon word 'hell', which comes from the verb 'to hele' or 'to hide'. This word is still used by gardeners today when they speak of 'heeling in' the roots of a plant, as they cover them with earth.

Those who arrive in hell will not be able to escape and will certainly be conscious of the awfulness of their surroundings. Jesus makes this quite clear in the story of the rich man and Lazarus, where the rich man in hell sees, speaks and feels regret as he recalls the past. This point is emphasised by the number of times Jesus says there will be 'wailing and gnashing of teeth'.

An awfully big adventure

Before we begin to look at heaven, we must first consider death from a Christian point of view. Victor Hugo's statement about the thoroughfare fails to give the sense of release, purpose and excitement that is always part of the New Testament word for death. In fact, after reading the New Testament you almost find yourself saying with James Barrie's Peter Pan, 'to die will be an awfully big adventure'.

Like Peter, the apostle Paul in his second letter to Timothy also speaks of the fact that the time for his 'departure' has come (2 Timothy 4:6). However, Paul uses the word *analusis* which conjures up three vivid pictures of death for the Christian.

It is a word which was used for the freeing of a slave. As the slave departs to freedom, you would hardly expect him to regard the event with morbid intro-spection. His mind, gripped by the experience of release, would race on to begin savouring the broad expanses of liberty. John Fletcher of Madeley under-stood this when he wrote: 'What is it to die but to open our eyes after the disagreeable dream of life. It is to break the prison of corrupt flesh and blood.'

In this century we see an example of the eagerness for the liberty death brings, in the last postcard of Dr F.B. Meyer. While lying ill at Boscombe, he addressed a postcard to Mr A. Lindsay Glegg with a very shaky hand. He said, 'I have raced you to Heaven, I am just off – see you there. Love, F.B. Meyer.'

How different this is from the attitude of those outside the Christian faith. As he lay dying on 5th June 1910, the American short-story writer O. Henry called to the nurse for a candle. When she asked why he wanted it, he replied, 'Because I am afraid to go home in the dark.'

This word 'departure' was also used by the philosophers for a problem that had been resolved. The problem had gone and the answer had come; intellectual light shone where there had been darkness. That is why Professor C.E.M. Joad once said that he was looking forward to death because it would bring the answer to many of the perplexing things that had puzzled him. Christians of every age have regarded death in this way. 'Now for the morning and the King's face. No more night and no more darkness', was the passionate cry of Donald Cargill just before he was martyred in Edinburgh in 1681.

The most interesting use of this word in the Bible is connected with shipping. *Analusis* is the word for the last rope to be cast off, thus freeing a ship to begin its journey. The vessel, having been held to the quay, is now free and her bows swing out towards the harbour mouth. Lord Tennyson used this figure of death in his poem 'Crossing the Bar'. The journey is not past but about to begin. The whole atmosphere of the word speaks of the excitement of adventure.

We must not forget that death is not a new route. This is the point Michael Green makes when he speaks of Vasco da Gama, the great Portuguese sailor, who was the first to circumnavigate the southernmost tip of Africa. As Vasco da Gama sailed around the Cape he changed its name from the 'Cape of Storms' to the 'Cape of Good Hope'. As Christians we take heart from the fact that Jesus has already died and has risen again: death has been circumnavigated.

Traveller, what lies over the hill?

As we turn to look at 'heaven' we echo George MacDonald's question 'traveller, what lies over the hill?' Reinhold Niebuhr said that 'it is unwise for Christians to claim any knowledge of either the furniture of heaven or of the temperature of hell'. Yet when we look at all Jesus says we find an amazing wealth of detail. It would be wrong to interpret the phrase, 'In my Father's house are many rooms' (John 14:2) to mean western-style housing with twentieth-century rooms. Dr Westcott begins to lead us back to the picture Jesus must have had in mind when he tells us that the word 'rooms' had the meaning of a resting place or a station on a great road where travellers found refreshment.

Archbishop Temple tells us that the word means a wayside caravanserai. A caravanserai was the motel for the camel caravans which crossed the great areas of the ancient world. A caravanserai probably consisted of a single building where the proprietor and his family lived. The main feature would have been space to park, with a watering place for the animals and somewhere to pitch a tent. If the caravanserai was in a desert, then it would have the atmosphere of an oasis, with trees providing shade from the relentless glare of the sun. At night, when all the guests had arrived and the animals were secured, a friendly, convivial spirit prevailed.

No admission except on business

When Florence Nightingale was told that a

loved one had died and gone 'to be at rest' she replied, 'Oh, no! I am sure the next life is immense activity.' That is the view of the New Testament too. Our hymn books often give us the idea of inactivity and boring repetition. Even in Heber's glorious hymn, 'Holy, Holy, Holy,' we seem to be condemned to endlessly 'casting down our golden crowns beside a glassy sea.' The New Testament view is that after death comes paradise, a fertile garden where the caravan comes to rest in the middle of a desert. It is a place where men and women are engaged in all the activities of recreation.

Your reservation

A caravan's progress across the desert was constantly hindered by slipping loads and escaping children, and therefore the prospect of the caravanserai would be even more eagerly awaited by the weary travellers. However, the vision of welcome and refreshment may well have been dulled by the depressing anxiety that the lateness of the arrival might mean a 'no vacancies' sign at the end of a hard day's journey. To ensure that this didn't happen, earlier in the day, the caravan master would send his servant on ahead to secure the appropriate reservations. This process of a secure place is also part of the teaching of Jesus, when He tells His disciples that He has gone ahead to prepare a place for them.

All roads do not lead to heaven

With so much detail it is surprising that the disciples wanted still more information. Perhaps it needed a doubter like Thomas to ask a necessary question and point to the one apparent flaw in all that Jesus had said. You can almost hear Thomas saying, 'We are glad that heaven is like a caravanserai and as real as a place on a map. We are delighted that our reservations are secure as if someone has personally gone ahead to book them. But how can we find the way to this heavenly resting place? There are neither roads nor signposts in a desert, much less on the way to heaven.'

Jesus replies, 'I am the way and the truth and the life. No one comes to the Father except through me' (John 14:6).

This remark quashes the illogical thought that all roads lead to heaven. Roads, after all, go in two directions both to and from the place we have in mind. So, once we have chosen the right road we must also choose the right direction. Jesus said that He is 'the Way', that is, the right road. He went on to say that He is 'the Truth', that is the right direction along the right road. He then added that He is 'the Life', so suggesting that He can give us the power to take us down the right road in the right direction. We can hardly ask for more than that.

Nothing profane shall enter in

Towards the end of the Bible we find a forceful reminder that must be included in any teaching on heaven. John tells us that nothing unclean will enter God's final kingdom (Revelation 21:27). Christianity is an ethical religion. It lays down a standard and teaches that one day we will be measured against it. Each action, every word uttered, will be measured against the divine yardstick. We may excuse ourselves for each failure, kind heaven may be forgiving, but even a cursory inward glance will tell us that we have fallen short of God's standard. As Isaiah says, with a quiet wit and wisdom, 'all our righteousnesses are as filthy rags' (Isaiah 64:6, AV).

The heart of the gospel is that in dying on

the cross for our sins, Jesus became our 'righteousness' (2 Corinthians 5:21) so that we might be allowed into heaven. Paul says 'if anyone is in Christ, he is a new creation' (2 Corinthians 5:17). Heaven is populated by those who have been made new by Jesus. For the Christian, judgement is therefore past and entrance to heaven is secured.

The last judgement

The apostle John, in his revelation, speaks of a 'great white throne' (Revelation 20:11), this is where the final judgement of sinners will take place. The followers of Christ will escape this, although they will have to stand before a 'judgement seat' (Romans 14:10), something quite separate and different. The word is *bema* and it describes the place where the judge stood at the ancient athletic games to watch the athletes competing and from where he would present rewards and prizes at the conclusion of the event. Every Christian will one day stand before the *bema* of Christ; their entrance into heaven is beyond doubt, but they will be rewarded according to how they have lived as Christians (*see* 1 Corinthians 3:12–15).

3

THE GREAT FEAST DAY ON THE ROAD TO FREEDOM

The Physical Experience

Dietrich Bonhoeffer, the German pastor executed by the Nazis on the day before World War II ended, called death 'the supreme festival on the road to freedom'. We will now look at the physical phenomena of death, and perhaps discover why Bonhoeffer regarded the day of his death like this.

The body stops working

In physical terms death takes place when the handful of chemicals which make up the physical apparatus of the human body cease to work. It is nothing less than a miracle that God has managed to breathe life into such a meagre handful of ordinary elements. If you take a wheelbarrow to your local chemist you will be able to buy all the ingredients for £95. You will need 3lb of calcium, 12oz of potassium, 8oz of sulphur, 2lb of phosphorus, 36lb of charcoal and a trace of sodium. If, on the way home, you pop into the ironmonger and buy a medium-size nail, and finally add 140lb of water you will have all the component chemicals that make up a human being. Only the miracle of life will be lacking.

It is easy to see why many people with little or no spiritual insight place such importance on the body. It is 'them', all they have, and consequently they do everything they can to protect and cultivate their bodies. However, the Christian's attitude should have a different emphasis.

Man wears God's image

God said, 'Let us make man wearing our own image and likeness'. This Knox translation of Genesis 1:26 emphasises, as the Hebrew does, that the word 'image' refers to the fact that God has shared His outward appearance with us. This immediately lifts us above the rest of the created world. There are also inward characteristics which God has shared with man. We have the power of thought, of feeling and of will. We are also like Him in that we are self-conscious and, to some degree, self-determining. Man, in the first place, even shared a moral likeness with God, because he was created good. Since the fall, when Adam and Eve chose to disobey God, his halo has slipped and, like the rest of creation, he is now scarred and marred by sin. In spite of this the Christian would want to say that man is so much more than Desmond Morris's 'vertical, hunting, weapon-toting, territorial, neotenous, brainy, Naked Ape, a primate by ancestry and a carnivore by adoption.'

Man is spirit

Having accomplished the redemption of the human race on the cross, Jesus cried out 'Father, into your hands I commit my spirit'. Notice that Jesus didn't say 'myself' or 'my body' but 'my spirit'. The spirit is the other side of man's nature and the side which needs to be 'born again'. If a developing relationship with God is to be encouraged, it is the spirit of man that needs to be nourished by worship and fed with the 'meat' of the Scriptures.

What actually happens when we die?

When the body ceases to function, *I* don't stop being *me*. When I die I leave this portable piece of plumbing behind and it either decomposes in the grave or is returned to dust and ashes by fire. Jesus said to the penitent thief, 'today you will be with me in paradise'. Socrates uttered a profound truth on his death bed when he said 'bury me if you can catch me'. All that can be caught is the empty container that had once held a human being.

It is undeniable that the human body can be very attractive. And when we are inhabiting them, as stewards, we have a responsibility to honour them, remembering always in whose 'image' we are made. There are few things, if any, more valuable than a human body when indwelt by a human being. But it is sentimentalism to carry this beyond the grave.

A clinical definition of death

Doctors are still debating an exact medical definition of death, so a layman is unlikely to come up with a definitive answer. For thousands of years death has been recognised by the failure of certain parts of the body. Until twenty years ago a man or a woman who had no pulse and who had ceased to breathe was said to be dead. Today various machines can deal with these failures, hence the concept of 'brain death', which is when the brain stem has ceased to function and artificial support to the other parts of the body becomes pointless. So today a clinical definition of death must include a recognition of brain death and not simply the failure of heart, lungs and kidneys, as in previous years.

The fear of death

The Victorians had a morbid fascination with death, but they hardly ever spoke about sex. Our generation appears to have reversed these subjects. However, the fear of death is universal. The Duke of Wellington said that 'a man must be a coward or a liar who could boast of never having felt a fear of death'. This is inevitable because, apart from Lazarus and one or two others on Easter day, no human being has been through death and come back again. Christians, however, do have the assurance that Jesus has 'destroyed death'. In the New Testament the word is *katargeo* and it literally means 'rendered ineffective'. We still have to face death and we may worry about the way it will come to us, but, because Jesus has made it ineffectual, death won't be able to hold us: that is the point.

Out-of-the-body experiences

The last few years have seen the increasing recognition of 'out-of-the-body experiences', often referred to simply as OBEs. People who have had serious accidents and been revived, or patients who have 'died' for a few moments on the operating table, while undergoing critical surgery, claim on recovery that they have had a glimpse of the afterlife.

In the 1970s a group of doctors arose who called themselves 'thanatologists' or those who 'study what happens after death'. Dr Raymond Moody wrote an international bestseller entitled *Life after Life*, in which he detailed hundreds of OBEs. Dr Moody is a Methodist and claims that his research neither proves nor disproves that there is life after death or that heaven and hell exist. Other writers on the subject are not so cautious. Dr Maurice Rawlings claims that OBEs prove the reality of Christianity, although some of the patients involved who have been resuscitated would repudiate this.

In *The Lion Book of Beliefs*, John Allan makes an important point in his section entitled 'Mysteries' when he says 'thanatological experiences "prove" very little. They afford grounds for fascinating speculation, but no more.' He concludes that 'it is hard to tell the exact moment at which someone passes from life to death' and therefore an OBE might be 'a fantasy conjured up by some region of the patient's brain.'

The popular newspapers continually run stories of those who claim to have died and come back from the dead. When these are brought to us for comment we must insist that there is no evidence for the reality of these claims, and they certainly don't add anything to all that the Scriptures have taught. The Bible must be the source of our doctrines and beliefs, rather than the writings of the sensation-seeking Press.

The end is the beginning

Before he was executed on 8th April 1945, Dietrich Bonhoeffer sent this message to George Bell, Bishop of Chichester: 'This is the end – but for me it is the beginning.' That is how Christians should look at death.

Wing-Commander Branse Burbridge won two DSOs and two DFCs for his night-fighter missions over Germany during World War II. His story was recorded in the bestseller *Night Fighter* by Rawnsley and Wright. Burbridge and Skelton, the two-man Mosquito crew, established a record number of enemy aircraft shot down by a night fighter. On every flight over Germany, and especially when engaging enemy aircraft in combat, they all took death into their own hands. This is how Branse Burbridge describes his first dog-fight:

In our first real scrap our opponent seemed to be out-turning me; I turned tighter than ever and banked very steeply – this 'toppled' the instruments, which would take 20 minutes to reset themselves. So even if he didn't get us first, we might spin into the sea... I felt prickly – I was afraid. Then something hit me, but it wasn't a bullet! In a split second, I realised two things: both stemmed from the fact that I was a Christian.

First, if God had further work for me to do for Him after the war, I was bound to survive; second, if I did get killed, death would be literally the gateway to heaven, and I should see the Lord Jesus Christ. So what did it matter?

The new life that Jesus Christ had given me is eternal, and so I need not be afraid of death. In fact, I have not been afraid since then. But it took that dog-fight at night over Germany to make me see this.

When I leave this earth I shall live eternal life in Christ's presence. While I'm here I live it 'at a distance'. Through it, He has taught me so many lessons, guided me through so many problems, given me so much satisfaction, spoken to me so often, that my belief in the living Christ could never be destroyed. Try telling a pilot at an overseas station that the RAF does not exist – and he'll tell you you're talking through your helmet!

Cancer – the rise of the crab

One problem that must be faced today is

the growing number of people who die as a result of cancer. The latest figures from the Office of Population Censuses and Surveys indicate that the trend of deaths from cancer over the past few years has been upwards, although the latest figures available for 1986 show a slight drop. In all, the numbers mean that few families will escape the disease in one form or another. A complication of cancer is the fear that surrounds the name. In America this is so great that euphemisms for cancer death are regularly used in newspaper reporting. Even in the astrological columns they print 'Crab' for 'Cancer' whilst the other eleven signs of the zodiac remain firmly in Latin. Fear can cause more harm than the disease. The wonders of modern medicine mean that much can be done, even complete cures achieved, if the disease is caught early enough. However, there is obviously some connection between the prevalence of the disease and our twentieth-century diet and lifestyle. Just as public opinion has been changed with regard to smoking, so we must now have a long hard look at other factors to see if they predispose us to cancer, and therefore contribute to early death.

The joy of dying

Final illness at the end of a long and happy life can hold the promise of a welcome release for many people. There are many among the elderly who approach death without any sense of apprehension. Indeed John Venn, to quote one famous case, was so filled with joy at the prospect of heaven that he actually lived an extra two weeks.

The greatest adventure of my life

James Casson was a young doctor who died in 1980. I heard him speak one Sunday morning at St Ebbes, Oxford and he tells his story in a little book called *The Greatest Adventure of My Life*. He says,

Dying makes life suddenly real. Watching my slow physical deterioration reaffirmed my belief that there is something else within, which would survive if only because my personality stayed the same in spite of the eroding bodily form in which it is confined... Strange to relate, however, my life as a practising Christian was changed by the knowledge that I was dying almost more than if I had been a committed atheist. Suddenly all I had been told or read in the Bible made sense. My lifestyle didn't change very much but my attitude did; it was as if I suddenly started really to live, although the reverse was true and I was dying. A clear spring morning is most meaningful after weeks of dull, wet weather. The slow build up of dust on a car windscreen goes unnoticed till I clean it with a few squirts of water and the windscreen wipers. So life can only really be understood when it is contrasted with death.

An understanding of death ought to sharpen our focus on life and make us want to enjoy every second until the moment when God takes us into eternity.

Suicide

A perplexing problem of our time is the rise in the number of suicides, especially among the young. There is no explicit prohibition in the Bible, although the implication is that God has 'fixed His cannon 'gainst self-slaughter' and therefore to take one's own life is usurping His authority in the matter of life and death. Most Christian thinking today would lay great stress on the mitigating factors of social and emotional stress. However, we must learn to have greater understanding, and to be more sensitive, as we seek to help the families and loved ones of suicide victims.

4

EASTER AND THE EASTERED

The Christian Experience

Easter is at the heart of Christianity with its teaching that Jesus rose from the dead. Take away this central truth and the whole of Christianity collapses into a myth. I will come back to this point later in the chapter when I touch on the historical evidence for the resurrection. Jesus is spoken of as one 'who has destroyed death and has brought life and immortality to light through the gospel' (2 Timothy 1:10). This makes the writers of the New Testament extremely bold when they come to write about the eternal life to be enjoyed by the Christian. Paul, for example, uses the past tense to speak of it in spite of the fact that we are still encumbered with a physical body which will one day have to die. Death is therefore an event we can approach without fear: it has 'lost its sting' and its power to hold us. One day, clothed in resurrection bodies, we will enter eternity to enjoy the presence of God for ever.

The dawning of a new day

To trace back the New Testament idea of life after death involves returning to the beginning of the Old Testament with its assumption that life continues beyond the grave: 'Then Abraham breathed his last and died at a good old age, an old man and full of years; and he was *gathered to his people*' (Genesis 25:8). Abraham was a great man of faith so you might expect him to be 'gathered to' God, but no – he is to be united with those of his family who lived before him in previous generations. The Old Testament scholar, Alec Motyer, commenting on the phrase 'gathered to his people', says 'the description as it stands is a telling revelation of the reality which life after death possessed for those ancient times. He (Abraham) went to join the company of those who had gone before.' Jacob had the same hope when he presumed that Joseph was dead and said

'In mourning will I go down to the grave to my son.'

Sheol

Sheol in the Old Testament is a place-name, and doesn't have the significance that words like 'hell' or 'heaven' have in the New Testament. It was the place everybody went to when they died. Murderers, thieves and adulterers went there but so did those who served God well. Alec Motyer says that 'while opinions may well differ in the interpretation of what the Old Testament tells about the *nature* of life in Sheol, there can be no disputing its insistence on the *fact* of life in Sheol.'

Old Testament men and women described difficult times as 'the snares of death' but death itself was never thought of as the end. During his life, David said to God 'You guide me with your counsel, and afterward you will take me into glory' (Psalm 73:24). A twentieth-century follower of Jesus Christ would not have to change those Old Testament words by one letter to describe his own certain hope for eternity.

For the men and women of the Old

Testament, Sheol was a place where spiritual and moral differences were preserved (e.g. Psalm 49). Those who had served God well could expect 'glory' and His enemies would expect adversity. Although the idea of adversity was not explicitly developed, there were occasional warnings of the dangers of entering the next world with sin unconfessed, unrepented, and therefore unforgiven. 'But man, despite his riches, does not endure; he is like the beasts that perish. This is the fate of those who trust in themselves' (Psalm 49:12,13).

The empty tomb

The most important of all the New Testament miracles is the resurrection of Jesus. Many people who have doubts about it have never stopped to consider the evidence. There have been several thorough studies of the facts by skilled lawyers who have examined the evidence much as they would in a court of law. The most famous of these lawyers is Frank Morison who wrote *Who Moved The Stone?* Another is Sir Norman Anderson, formerly Professor of Oriental Laws and Director of the

Institute of Advanced Legal Studies in the University of London, who wrote *The Evidence For The Resurrection.* We must be honest about the evidence and admit that it can only bring us to the place where we say, 'there is a very high degree of possibility that Jesus rose from the dead.' What brings the final conviction of certainty for most people is to meet the risen Jesus. This is what it means to be a Christian, to experience the cleansing from sin that He offers, and to begin the new life He makes available to those who follow Him. Let us look at a few of the details of the resurrection.

Jesus spoke openly about it

When Jesus first spoke to the Jews in picture language about His being raised up 'in three days', (John 2:19) they misunderstood Him and thought He was referring to Herod's Temple. They replied 'It has taken forty-six years to build this temple, and you are going to raise it in three days?' It was only after the resurrection had taken place that the disciples recalled what He had said (John 2:22).

From the moment Peter made his great confession of faith at Caesarea Philippi, 'You are the Christ, the Son of the living God' (Matt. 16:16), Jesus began to explain to His disciples about the things which would take place in Jerusalem; how He would suffer at the hands of the elders and chief priests and be put to death, but 'on the third day be raised to life' (Matthew 16:21).

When they got back to Galilee He told them this again (Matt. 17:23) and then on the way to Jerusalem He told them once more (Matt. 20:19). As Sir Norman Anderson says, 'It seems incontrovertible that Christ Himself foretold His crucifixion and resurrection.'

He died

Fundamental to any teaching on the resurrection is the need to establish that Jesus actually died: he didn't merely faint, as some Muslims teach, or merely appear to die. When Joseph of Arimathea asked Pilate for permission to bury the body of Jesus, 'Pilate was surprised to hear that He was already dead. Summoning the centurion, he asked him if Jesus had already died.' The centurion confirmed that He had. There were several eye witnesses of His death. It is highly improbable that anyone could survive crucifixion, especially if they had experienced violent flogging beforehand, as Jesus had. The body of Jesus was bandaged for the tomb and this process required the use of 34 kilograms (75lb) of ointment (John 19:39). If Jesus hadn't died on the cross He would certainly have suffocated as His body was prepared for the grave.

The historical reality of the resurrection

Although no one actually witnessed the resurrection taking place, there were many who saw Jesus after the event. Some saw the place where His body had been laid with the still folded but empty and, therefore, collapsed shroud still there. Others confirmed that they saw the Jesus they knew eating, walking and talking. On one occasion the risen Jesus was seen by a group of over five hundred disciples. Indeed the appearance of the resurrected Jesus conquered the uncertainty and fear of one doubting disciple and turned the rest of the frightened, retiring group into a company of men who preached Jesus and His resurrection to the ends of the known world.

If Jesus didn't rise from the dead?

If the resurrection of Jesus didn't take place then there is only one conclusion to be drawn: Christians are a deluded people who have misled millions of others for the past 2,000 years. Paul expresses this clearly when he says, 'if Christ has not been raised, our preaching is useless and so is your faith. More than that, we are then found to be false witnesses about God' (1 Corinthians 15:14,15).

The prototype

The argument of the New Testament is that Jesus did come back from the tomb and that He is therefore the prototype of a new man (1 Corinthians 15:20–23).

The problem of sleep

One problem that arises here could be

called the 'problem of sleep'. Death may seem to be the start of an exciting voyage to some, but to others it is clearly a false start, because before the ship reaches the harbour limit they feel it is whisked into a dry-dock and may have to wait a million years before the voyage can continue. They would say that after death we sleep until Christ comes, before we actually go to enjoy heaven. Such a view is encouraged by our word 'cemetery' which comes from the Greek word meaning 'sleeping place'.

When we turn to the New Testament we certainly find that Paul makes some reference to 'those who have fallen asleep' (1 Cor. 15:20). One obvious reason for this would be Paul's Jewish background: the time before he became a Christian would have provided him with a view of survival after death that was closely akin to sleep. It is likely that he was simply making a statement about death that was so strongly coloured with Old Testament thought that it had the effect of overriding any other picture within the word.

On the other hand, the New Testament speaks clearly of immediate resurrection after death. Jesus said to the penitent thief as they were both dying after crucifixion, 'today you will be with me in paradise'

(Luke 23:43). To encourage us, the writer to the Hebrews tells us that we are 'surrounded by such a great cloud of witnesses' (Hebrews 12:1). There is a problem here in the New Testament and we must acknowledge that there is. Probably the answer has to do with time and eternity. It would be possible for two people to die millions of years apart and both immediately after death step into eternity at precisely the same moment. Eternity is not restricted by time.

The question of sleep remains a problem but it would present an even greater difficulty to find a doctrine of a bodiless soul in the Bible. On balance the New Testament says that when we make our *exodus* or departure we go straight to paradise.

The resurrection of the believer

The Bible does not appear to predict a general resurrection of the dead, but teaches rather that there will be a definite moment in time when Jesus will come to take His Church to heaven. This will include all who have trusted in Him and who have died in the faith (1 Thessalonians

4:13–18). Jesus says that this group will 'rise to live' (John 5:29) and enjoy 'eternal life' having 'crossed over from death to life' (John 5:24).

Then those outside Him will 'rise to be condemned' (John 5:29) and 'judged according to what they have done' (Revelation 20:12). The teaching of Scripture is that no one in the first group will be lost and no one in the second will be saved.

An answer to the riddle of life

Sigmund Freud wrote, 'And finally there is the painful riddle of death, for which no remedy at all has yet been found, nor probably ever will be.' According to Christian teaching that is patently not true. The answer to the riddle of death is to be found in Christ. It is not a question of doing good things or believing the right teaching but having a living, personal faith that Jesus paid the penalty for our sins by His death on the cross, enabling us to be reconciled with God and to have eternal life. If we believe in Him in this way, then at our burial or cremation our bodies will be sown into the ground as a 'perishable' seed and will be 'raised imperishable' (1

Cor. 15:42); it will be 'sown a natural body' and 'raised a spiritual body' (1 Cor. 15:44). It won't be the same body or even a reconstruction of the various parts, but it will be recognisable as *our* body and there will be continuity with the past, rather as a grain of wheat that is planted eventually becomes a full grown stalk and ear.

Being Eastered ourselves

The New Testament writers not only speak of the resurrection of Jesus in the past tense but also of the believer. What they appear to be stressing is that our future resurrection is so real and definite that there is a sense in which it has already taken place. In his letter to the Christians in Ephesus Paul uses three verbs translated into three English phrases to describe what has happened to the believer once he accepts Christ. He says God has 'made us alive with Christ', 'raised us up with Christ' and 'seated us with Him in the heavenly realms'. John Stott says 'what excites our amazement, however, is that now Paul is not talking about Christ but *about us*. He is affirming not that God quickened, raised and seated Christ, but that He has quickened, raised and seated us with Christ.'

The great distinctive characteristic of God's redeemed people pictured in Paul's letter to the Ephesians is not that they admire and worship Jesus, or live according to a new standard, or believe in a dynamically different way, but that, because of their being 'in Christ', they have actually begun to share in the ascension, resurrection and exaltation of Jesus. John Stott continues,

> Moreover, this talk about the solidarity with Christ in His resurrection and exaltation is not a piece of meaningless Christian mysticism. It bears witness to a living experience that Christ has given us on the one hand a new life (with a sensitive awareness of the reality of God, and a love for Him and for His people) and on the other a new victory (with evil increasingly under our feet). We were dead, but have been made spiritually alive and alert. We were in captivity, but have been enthroned.

This, surely is, what Gerard Manley Hopkins was referring to when he urges us to let Christ 'easter in us'.

5

MEDITATION AMONG THE TOMBS

The Historical Event

There used to be a famous book entitled *Meditation Among the Tombs* by Hervey, which I have seen in many second-hand book catalogues, although I have never actually handled a copy myself. Hervey's theme, the very end of people's lives, is neither morbid nor unusual. In older libraries you will find a whole shelf on this subject which will include such volumes as Andrew Bonar's *The Last Day of Eminent Christians,* and *Death in Art and Epigram* by F. Parkes Webber. To take one of these books from the shelf and begin to read is far from depressing. Indeed, even a hurried glance will reveal men and women who, on the threshold of death, were able to say, with Mr Despondency in *Pilgrim's Progress,*

'Farewell night, welcome day'. A German proverb says, 'He that begins to live begins to die.' What these books reveal is that some men and women have discovered the secret of turning death into life.

Last words

Catherine Booth (1829–1890) After her marriage to the founder of the Salvation Army, William Booth, Catherine spent a good deal of her time seeking to improve the position of women and children in society. She was a gifted speaker in her own right. She wasn't a strong child and in her last years she suffered with cancer. Her last words were,

> The waters are rising, but so am I. I'm not going under but over. Do not be concerned about dying: go on living well, the dying will be right.

John Bunyan (1628–1688) The tinker of Bedford, who gave the world one of the great Christian classics, *Pilgrim's Progress*, said as he died,

Weep not for me, but for yourselves. I go to the Father of our Lord Jesus Christ; who will, no doubt, through the mediation of His eternal Son, receive me, though a sinner; when I hope we shall meet ere long to sing a new song, and remain everlastingly happy, world without end, Amen.

William Carey (1761–1834) The father of the modern missionary movement was a shoemaker who so applied himself to study while repairing shoes that by the time he was twenty he could read the Bible in six languages. He went on to spend over forty-one years on the mission field in India, and was directly responsible for translating portions of the Bible into thirty-six languages and dialects. His last words were,

When I am gone, say nothing about Dr Carey; speak about Dr Carey's Saviour.

John Wesley (1703–1791) The founder of Methodism started his working life as assistant to his father at the Parish Church in Epworth before going as a missionary to Georgia in the United States. He returned from there after three years thoroughly discouraged and broken in health.

Through Moravians working in London he found the experience of full assurance of salvation on 24th May 1738. From that moment he became a travelling preacher covering 250,000 miles, mainly on horseback, and preaching over 40,000 sermons. He was a prolific writer, preacher and organiser. He died in London after a short illness in 1791. He was almost eighty-eight years old. Twice in the last few moments of his life he cried out in triumph, '*The best of all is, God is with us.*' His very last word was '*Farewell!*'

John Newton (1725–1807) Today, this gifted preacher and hymn writer, is widely known as the author of *Amazing Grace*. Few lives, if any, reflect more amazing grace than his own: he changed from a hard-swearing sailor to a vicious West African slave trader, and then became a Christian, eventually becoming a leading evangelical in the Church of England, and influencing such people as William Wilberforce and Hannah Moore. He died in his eighty-second year. His last words were,

> I am like a person going on a journey in a stage coach, who expects its arrival every hour, and is frequently looking out

of the window for it . . . I am packed and sealed, and ready for the post.

D.L. Moody (1837–1899) The first evangelist of modern times under whose preaching and the singing of Ira D. Sankey, hundreds of thousands, if not millions, became Christians. His last words were, 'I see earth receding; heaven is opening. God is calling me.'

Francis Schaeffer (1912–1984) One of the foremost Christian apologists of the twentieth century, he started his working life as a part-time wet-fish salesman in America and went on to popularise philosophy and establish the L'Abri study centre in Switzerland. While seriously ill with cancer, he managed a mammoth tour linked with his last book *The Great Evangelical Disaster*. He died at home in Rochester, Minnesota on 15th May 1984, with his family. They remembered him saying frequently during his last days, 'His grace is sufficient.'

Martin Lloyd-Jones (1899–1981) This gifted expositor and preacher followed Campbell Morgan as the minister of Westminster Chapel in London. He was probably one of the greatest influences on the Christian Church in the twentieth century through his preaching, writing and his work among students. In February 1981, recognising that his earthly task was finished, he ended his treatment, cancelled his papers from 28th February, and said to his family 'Don't pray for healing' adding, 'don't try to hold me back from glory.' He died peacefully in his sleep the next day, 1st March 1981.

Martyrs

The word 'martyr' can easily conjure up an image of a bygone age and heroic men and women in old-fashioned costumes being burned at the stake for their faith. Since Stephen, the first Christian martyr, laid down his life many have been called to follow his example. Yet, on examination, the facts and figures of martyrdom are surprising in their suggestion that the number of people that have died for their allegiance to Jesus Christ in the twentieth century is greater than the combined totals of every other century.

I thought about this a little while ago when I met Elizabeth Elliot, whose husband was martyred on 8th January 1956. Many people of my generation were moved by the death of Jim Elliot, Nate Saint, Pete Fleming, Ed McCully and Roger Youderian as they determined to take the message of Jesus to the Auca Indians, a tribe living in the jungles of Ecuador who appeared to have had no contact with the outside world. In a spirit true to the New Testament Elizabeth Elliot took up the work for which her husband had laid down his life and went back unarmed with a tiny daughter to continue the work of trying to win the Aucas to the Christian faith. The fact that she was willing to do this probably accounted for the first Auca becoming a Christian.

Looking at martyrs in history is rather like looking at the deathbed scenes early in this chapter: rather than being depressing, it is exhilarating to see the faith and courage of these men and women who, instead of playing safe, were willing to chance death so that others might believe.

Here is a handful of examples, just a few of many stirring stories.

Jim Elliot (martyred 8th January 1956) On Tuesday 3rd January 1956 Jim Elliot and his four companions were up at dawn checking their equipment and the small plane that was to fly them into Auca territory. At 7a.m. they had a time of prayer and sang their favourite hymn 'We Rest on Thee'. On the last verse their voices rang with deep conviction.

> We rest on Thee, our Shield and our
>   Defender,
> Thine is the battle, Thine shall be the
>   praise;
> When passing through the gates of pearly
>   splendour
> Victors, we rest with Thee through endless
>   days.

They had already spotted what they thought would be a safe landing area on a firm sand-bar next to a river. They called this 'Palm Beach' and landed safely there, establishing their base camp.

On Friday a group of Auca Indians arrived at the camp and were given trinkets and a machete, together with a model of the plane. A woman Auca, who the men called 'Delilah', enjoyed looking at a copy of *Time*. They even took one of the Auca men for a flight over his own village.

Saturday was an anticlimax: the men

waited with high hopes but not one of the Auca Indians appeared again. At 4.30 a.m. on 8th January, Marj Saint, for the wives, switched on her radio to contact the men, expecting to hear that the Aucas had taken them to their village. There was no radio response from 'Palm Beach'. Just silence. They didn't know it at the time, but the men were already dead, killed by the lethal lances that all Auca men carried for both hunting and settling arguments. The diaries of several of the men revealed that they had thought about the possibility of death and were even willing for this, if the Aucas could be won for Christ. Indeed, the pilot, Nate Saint, had broadcast on the missionary radio station HCJB,

God Himself laid down the law when he built the universe. He knew when He made it what the price was going to be. God didn't hold back His only Son, but gave Him up to pay the price for our failure and sin. Missionaries constantly face expendability. Jesus said, 'There is no man that hath left house, or brethren, or sisters, or mother, or wife, or children, or lands for My sake and the Gospel's but shall not receive an hundredfold now in this time and in the world to come eternal life.'

Stephen (martyred AD 33) With his willingness
to serve, Stephen responded to the cry of
help as men were needed to relieve the
more menial tasks of the leaders of the
early Church, freeing them to concentrate
on prayer and preaching (Acts 6:1). Acts 6
describes how the young Church required
spiritually qualified men to undertake the
most practical and menial jobs. It could
have been his willingness to serve, as well
as the fact that he was 'full of the Spirit,
wisdom, faith, grace and power' (Acts
6:3,5 and 8) that enabled Stephen to move
quickly to the place where he too was able
to concentrate on preaching and teaching.
Very soon his public ministry was being
opposed by the authorities in the synagogue,
and they tried to silence him. He was
arrested and made to appear before the
Sanhedrin, the Jewish parliament. In
reply to the charge of blasphemy, Stephen
preached a sermon on God's dealings with
His people since Abraham. In a bold and
masterful way he showed how it was the
Jewish authorities who were wrong and
not the young Church. 'Stephen, full of the
Holy Spirit, looked up to heaven and saw
the glory of God, and Jesus standing at the
right hand of God' (Acts 7:55). The
authorities then 'covered their ears and,

yelling at the top of their voices, they all rushed at him, dragged him out of the city and began to stone him.' Stephen 'fell on his knees and cried out, "Lord, do not hold this sin against them." When he had said this, he fell asleep.' (Acts 7:57, 60).

Polycarp (martyred 23rd February AD 156) Polycarp was the senior pastor of the Church in Smyrna at the beginning of the second century. In AD 156 a sudden upsurge of persecution led by the Jews meant that eleven Christians were seized, tortured and thrown to wild animals. At the end of this orgy of bestiality the crowd clamoured for the leader of the Christian Church to be arrested and punished. Polycarp was discovered on a farm outside the city, where he had refused to make any attempt to conceal his identity. He was arrested, and while food was set before his captors he spent the time in prayer. The arresting party then set out for the stadium in Smyrna. On their arrival the vast crowd went wild. Somehow, above the noise, a voice rang out with the encouraging words, 'Be strong, Polycarp, and play the man.' The crowd demanded that Polycarp should be thrown to the beasts. The proconsul tried to persuade him to swear an oath of allegiance to Caesar which would give him immediate freedom. He refused with the memorable words, 'For eighty-six years I have served Him, and He has never failed me: How can I revile my King and my Saviour?' On the grounds that the games were officially over, the proconsul refused the mob's request for Polycarp to be given to the animals. Instead he ordered that he should die by fire. Such was the bitterness of the Jews towards Christians that they broke their sabbath commandment in hurrying to gather wood. Finally Polycarp was tied to the stake and the fire lit, but the wind seemed to bend the flames around and above him. Polycarp prayed and a soldier used his sword to end the pastor's ordeal. So, on 23rd February AD 156 the Christian Church in Smyrna knew what it meant to suffer for their faith. They also had a perfect example of the gentle spirit of witness and praise that could be theirs if they were called to walk the way of the martyr.

Nicholas Ridley (martyred 16th October 1555)
J.C. Ryle says that the name Nicholas Ridley 'ought to be a household word mongst true hearted Englishmen.' Cer-

tainly in the ranks of the Reformers no one deserves a higher place than Ridley. Born in Northumberland near the Scottish border about 1500, he was educated at a local school in Newcastle upon Tyne and Cambridge University. On graduation in 1524 he became a Fellow of his College, Pembroke, and eventually its Master in 1540. In the same year he was appointed Chaplain to Henry VIII. He became Bishop of London in 1550 and was nominated as the Bishop of Durham. The death of the young King Edward VI halted Ridley's promotion in the Church of England. Indeed, Queen Mary so disliked his theology that he was an exception to her amnesty and was immediately confined to the Tower of London. He was taken from there to Oxford in 1554 to be insulted at a mock trial and finally burned at the stake with Hugh Latimer on 16th October 1555. The Martyrs Memorial in Oxford marks the site. When the fire was lit at Ridley's feet, Hugh Latimer said 'Be of good comfort, Master Ridley, and play the man. We shall this day light such a candle, by God's grace in England, as I trust shall never be put out.'

Playing the man

Christians down the ages have 'played the man' while facing death in a variety of circumstances. Relatively few have been martyred, many more ravaged by illness, some have faced the horrors of war, but most have been ordinary people facing life's natural end. Simply to trace the facts of the few that we know about has been an inspiration to me. Perhaps the greatest pleasure has been to see the way that the evidence for Christ's resurrection has been underlined time and again.

The door that cannot be shut again

C.S. Lewis put it so clearly.

> Jesus has forced open a door that had been locked since the death of the first man. He has met, fought, and beaten the king of death. Everything is different because He has done so. This is the beginning of a new creation. The New Testament doesn't explain the resurrection of Jesus. But His resurrection certainly explains the New Testament.

I have gone home

On the slopes of a mountain in Kenya is a simple grave. The Dean and Chapter of Westminster Abbey had offered a place for the body of the Chief Scout, Lord Baden-Powell, between the graves of the Unknown Warrior and David Livingstone. But after consideration, the family declined the offer, and had him buried in the Kenya he loved with a guard of honour consisting of Boy Scouts from Africa, Europe and Asia. The simple stone that marks the grave has on it a carved circle with a dot in the centre – the Scout trail sign: 'I have gone home'. For the believer it couldn't be expressed more eloquently than that. In itself it is a reminder that before we go home we need to get to know the Father and the family. And doing just that, becoming a twentieth-century follower of Jesus Christ, is the secret of 'playing the man' both in life and in the face of death.

Other titles in the Foundations series

He Saves

R T Kendall

In *He Saves*, an outstanding Gospel teacher looks at every aspect of the Bible's teaching on salvation and the Christian's experience of it in everyday life. Writing with directness and energy, Dr Kendall conveys the excitement of the good news of salvation, emphasising that we are saved by faith alone, and not by works.

He Saves is a clear and powerful explanation for those who are seeking, and for new and uncertain Christians. It will also help mature Christians return to basics.

'Dr Kendall brushes the cobwebs off theological terminology and simply answers the questions: How do I become a Christian? How do I know that I am a Christian?' *Christian Bookseller*

He Gives Us Signs

Gerald Coates

Does God still heal today? Is his healing power manifested in the physical world (miraculous healing of specific physical ailments) or is it in the spiritual realm (the healing of our relationship with God through Christ)?

Gerald Coates examines the 'signs and wonders' teaching and movement of recent times, describing how his own attitudes have developed during his ministry.

Kingdom Life

Martin Goldsmith

'The kingdom' is a popular subject among evangelical Christians, but confusion abounds as to the definition of 'the kingdom' and what 'kingdom living' really means. Some attach the label 'kingdom' to the revival of signs and wonders today; others think that 'the kingdom' is all about the future.

But God's kingdom is a far richer and more significant reality – past, present and future – than these narrow definitions allow, argues Martin Goldsmith in this challenging overview. Using his Jewish knowledge of the Old Testament concept of the kingdom, he explores the full richness of the kingdom that John the Baptist heralded and Jesus Christ ushered in, applying his insights to Christian living today.

'This little book provides a sweeping introduction to the Bible's teaching on the Kingdom of God and the relevance of that teaching to current controversies.'
Christian Weekly Newspapers

He Brings Us Together

Clive Calver

He Brings Us Together traces the roots of evangelical belief and practice, sketches a short history of the movement to the present day, and calls for allegiance to the Bible and a commitment to social action and unity. This book is designed to encourage evangelicals to recognise their identity, their distinctiveness and their common ground with one another across the denominational spectrum.

He Guides Us

Jonathan Lamb

He Guides Us affirms that God does guide the lives of individual Christians precisely and effectively. At the heart of the subject of guidance lies the greatest privilege – knowing God.

This book discusses *how* God guides: through the Bible, fellow Christians, circumstances, gifts, prophecy, dreams and visions. It provides valuable help in discerning God's will and identifying his voice.

He Tells Us To Go

Ian Coffey

Ian Coffey sets out to define what evangelism really
means: who it is aimed at, what the Bible says, and
leaves unsaid. He asks whether this highly emotive and
often misunderstood subject is a twentieth-century
phenomenon of mass meetings, or a strictly one-to-one
affair. *He Tells Us To Go* also discusses the relationship of
evangelism to social action, to the ecumenical
movement, and to other religions.

Gets to grips with awkward questions. A very helpful
little booklet.

He Gives His Word

Ian Barclay

The Bible is the essential basis for Christian belief: it is
particularly important to evangelicals. Too many take
it for granted, however, and Ian Barclay challenges
common assumptions held, and explains what the Bible
is all about: its relevance, authorship, interpretations
and apparent contradictions. He demonstrates the
continuing centrality of the Bible and the fact that it still
speaks directly to Christians today.